Manifesting Money Mastery

Discover How to Manifest Money to Unlock Your Financial Potential, Transform Your Mindset, and Create a Life of Abundance

Jeff Hill

CONTENTS

Welcome to "Manifesting Money Mastery: Discover How to Manifest Money to Unlock Your Financial Potential, Transform Your Mindset, and Create a Life of Abundance." In this transformative journey, we will explore the principles, practices, and mindset necessary to attract financial abundance into your life. Whether you are seeking to overcome financial challenges, increase your wealth, or align your financial goals with your purpose, this book will serve as your guide.

Money is an essential aspect of our lives, providing us with opportunities, security, and the ability to create the life we desire. Yet, many of us struggle to manifest the financial abundance we crave. We may be burdened by limiting beliefs, unconscious patterns, and a scarcity mindset that hold us back from realizing our true potential.

But here's the truth: You have the power to rewrite your financial story. You possess the ability to shift your mindset, align your energy, and take inspired action to manifest money and create a life of abundance.

"Manifesting Money Mastery" is designed to be a comprehensive roadmap, offering you the tools, techniques, and insights to unlock your financial potential. We will delve into the art of manifestation, exploring the power of thoughts, emotions, and believes in shaping your financial reality. You will learn how to reprogram your subconscious mind, release money blocks, and cultivate a positive money mindset that supports your journey towards abundance.

Throughout this book, we will explore practical steps you can take to attract financial prosperity. From budgeting and financial planning to building multiple streams of income and investing wisely, we will equip you with the knowledge and strategies to create a solid foundation for your financial success.

But manifesting money goes beyond mere practicality. It involves aligning with universal laws, embracing the energy of abundance, and tapping into your intuition to seize opportunities. We will explore techniques such as visualization, affirmations, and creating powerful money manifestation rituals that amplify your intention and create a magnetic field for financial abundance.

However, manifesting money is not a solitary pursuit. It is intertwined with personal growth, relationships, and making a positive impact on the world. We will delve into the importance of giving back, cultivating a holistic approach to abundance, and celebrating your financial successes as part of a larger journey towards a purposeful and fulfilling life.

As we embark on this transformative journey together, it is essential to remember that manifesting money is not about greed or selfishness. It is about embracing the inherent abundance of the universe, recognizing your worthiness of financial prosperity, and using your resources to create a positive ripple effect in your life and the lives of others.

So, are you ready to unlock the abundance code and embark on a journey of financial transformation? Let's begin. Open your mind, open your heart, and prepare to manifest the money and create the life of abundance you deserve.

CHAPTER 1: INTRODUCTION TO MANIFESTING MONEY

Money has always played a significant role in our lives. It provides us with the means to meet our needs, pursue our dreams, and create a life of comfort and security. However, many people struggle with money, experiencing financial limitations and scarcity.

What if I told you that you have the power to change your financial reality? That you can manifest money and create abundance in your life? In this chapter, we will explore the concept of manifesting money and how it can transform your relationship with wealth.

Understanding the Power of Manifestation

Manifestation is the process of bringing something into existence through focused intention and belief. When it comes to money, manifestation involves aligning your thoughts, emotions, and actions with abundance to attract financial prosperity into your life. The power to manifest money lies within your ability to harness the energy of the universe and direct it towards your financial goals.

Dispelling Myths and Misconceptions About Money

Before diving into the manifestation process, it's important to address common myths and misconceptions that can hinder your progress. Some of these myths include beliefs like "money is the root of all evil" or "wealth is only for the lucky few." By debunking these limiting beliefs and replacing them with empowering perspectives, you create a fertile ground for financial abundance to flourish.

The Connection Between Mindset and Abundance

Your mindset plays a critical role in manifesting money. Your thoughts, beliefs, and attitudes about money shape your experiences and the opportunities that come your way. By cultivating a mindset of abundance, you shift your focus from scarcity to limitless possibilities. This mindset shift allows you to attract financial abundance and create a positive relationship with money.

By the end of this chapter, you will have gained a clear understanding of the power of manifestation, debunked limiting beliefs, and recognized the role of mindset in attracting financial abundance. Get ready to embark on a transformative journey that will revolutionize your relationship with money. The power to manifest money is within your grasp, and it's time to unlock your financial potential.

CHAPTER 2: SETTING FINANCIAL GOALS

To manifest money effectively, it's crucial to establish clear and compelling financial goals. Setting goals provides a direction for your manifestation efforts and gives you a roadmap to follow. In this chapter, we will explore the process of setting financial goals that align with your desires and aspirations.

Identifying Your Financial Desires and Aspirations

To manifest money effectively, it's important to identify your specific financial goals and desires. Take the time to reflect on what you truly want to achieve with your finances. Do you aspire to achieve financial independence, travel the world, start a business, or support your family? Clearly defining your financial desires sets the foundation for a successful manifestation.

Creating SMART Goals

Once you have identified your financial desires, transform them into SMART goals. SMART stands for Specific, Measurable, Achievable, Relevant, and Time-bound. By setting specific and measurable goals, you provide clarity to the universe and create a roadmap for your manifestation journey.

Ensure your goals are achievable and relevant to your financial aspirations, and set a realistic deadline for their attainment.

Visualizing Your Ideal Financial Future

Visualization is a powerful tool in manifesting money. Take the time to vividly imagine your ideal financial future. Picture yourself living in abundance, experiencing financial freedom, and enjoying the lifestyle you desire. Engage all your senses and immerse yourself in this visualization exercise. By creating a clear mental image of your desired financial reality, you align your energy with abundance.

By the end of this chapter, you will have learned the importance of setting financial goals, how to transform your desires into SMART goals, and the power of visualization in manifesting money. With clear goals in place, you will have a strong foundation for the manifestation process and be well on your way to attracting the financial abundance you desire.

CHAPTER 3: CULTIVATING A PROSPERITY MINDSET

In the journey of manifesting money, developing a prosperity mindset is crucial. Your mindset shapes your beliefs, thoughts, and actions, which in turn influence your financial outcomes. In this chapter, we will explore the essential steps to cultivate a prosperity mindset and overcome limiting beliefs that may be blocking your abundance.

Unleashing the Power of Positive Thinking

Positive thinking is essential in manifesting money. By consciously focusing on positive thoughts and beliefs about money, you create a magnetic field that attracts prosperity. Practice affirmations that reinforce abundance, wealth, and financial success. Replace negative self-talk with empowering statements that affirm your ability to manifest money.

Overcoming Limiting Beliefs and Scarcity Mentality

Limiting beliefs and a scarcity mentality can block your ability to manifest money. Common limiting beliefs include thoughts like "I'm not worthy of wealth" or "There's never enough money." Identify these limiting beliefs and challenge them. Replace them with empowering beliefs such as "I am deserving of abundance" or "Money flows easily and abundantly into my life." Cultivate a mindset that embraces the limitless possibilities of financial abundance.

Practicing Gratitude and Abundance Consciousness

Gratitude is a powerful tool for shifting your focus from lack to abundance. Develop a daily gratitude practice where you express gratitude for the money you have, as well as the abundance in other areas of your life. Embrace an abundance consciousness by acknowledging the abundance that already exists in your life. Celebrate even the smallest financial wins and appreciate the opportunities that come your way.

By the end of this chapter, you will have learned how to harness the power of positive thinking, overcome limiting beliefs, and cultivate gratitude and abundance consciousness. These practices will lay the foundation for a prosperity mindset that magnetically attracts money and opportunities into your life. Prepare to embrace a mindset of abundance and unlock the limitless possibilities for financial manifestation.

CHAPTER 4: CLEARING MONEY BLOCKS

In our journey towards manifesting money, it's essential to address any subconscious money blocks that may be holding us back. These blocks can be deeply ingrained beliefs and patterns that sabotage our financial success. In this chapter, we will explore techniques to identify and clear money blocks, allowing for the free flow of abundance in our lives.

Identifying and Releasing Subconscious Money Blocks

Subconscious money blocks are deep-rooted beliefs and patterns that sabotage your financial success. Engage in self-reflection and introspection to identify these blocks. Explore your past experiences, childhood upbringing, and societal conditioning that may have contributed to these blocks. Once identified, release them by using techniques such as affirmations, visualization, and energy healing.

Healing Past Traumas and Negative Experiences With Money

Past traumas and negative experiences related to money can create emotional barriers to abundance. Engage in healing practices to release these emotional wounds. Inner child healing, forgiveness exercises, and energy healing modalities like Reiki or EFT (Emotional Freedom Techniques) can be powerful tools for healing and letting go of negative associations with money.

Utilizing Affirmations and Visualization Techniques

Affirmations and visualization help reprogram your subconscious mind for abundance. Create positive affirmations that reinforce your financial goals and repeat them daily. Visualize yourself living in abundance, experiencing financial success, and achieving your desired lifestyle. Engage all your senses in this visualization practice to make it more vivid and impactful.

By the end of this chapter, you will have gained insights into identifying and releasing subconscious money blocks, healing past traumas, and incorporating affirmations and visualization techniques into your manifestation practice. As you clear these blocks, you create a fertile ground for financial abundance to flow effortlessly into your life. Get ready to unleash your true financial potential by addressing and overcoming the obstacles that have been holding you back.

CHAPTER 5: ALIGNING WITH ABUNDANCE

To manifest money successfully, it's crucial to align yourself with the frequency of abundance. In this chapter, we will explore the universal laws of attraction and abundance and learn how to align our thoughts, emotions, and actions to attract financial prosperity.

Understanding the Universal Laws of Attraction and Abundance

The Law of Attraction states that like attracts like. By aligning your thoughts, emotions, and actions with abundance, you attract financial prosperity. The Law of Abundance reminds you that the universe is limitless in its offerings and there is more than enough for everyone. Embrace these universal laws and align your energy with abundance.

Harnessing the Law of Vibration and Resonance

Everything in the universe is energy, including money. Raise your vibrational frequency to align with the frequency of abundance. Cultivate positive emotions like joy, gratitude, and love. Engage in activities that bring you happiness and fulfillment. Surround yourself with positive people and environments. As you raise your energetic resonance, you attract financial abundance.

Taking Inspired Action and Leveraging Opportunities

Manifesting money requires more than just positive thinking; it involves taking inspired action. Be proactive in seeking opportunities that align with your financial goals. Take calculated risks and step out of your comfort zone. Be open to receiving and acting upon opportunities that come your way. Trust your intuition and seize the chances that lead to financial growth.

By the end of this chapter, you will have gained a deeper understanding of the universal laws of attraction and abundance, learned how to raise your vibrational frequency, and discovered the importance of taking inspired action. Aligning yourself with abundance creates a powerful magnetism that draws financial opportunities and prosperity into your life. Get ready to embrace the flow of abundance and step into a new level of financial manifestation.

CHAPTER 6: MONEY MANIFESTATION TECHNIQUES

In this chapter, we will explore practical techniques and rituals that can amplify your money manifestation efforts. These techniques harness the power of intention, visualization, and focused energy to manifest money in your life.

Creating a Powerful Money Manifestation Ritual

Design a personalized money manifestation ritual that incorporates elements that resonate with you. This ritual can include practices such as affirmations, visualization, lighting candles or incense, using crystals, and creating a sacred space. Engage in this ritual regularly, preferably daily, to amplify your intention and create a strong energetic container for manifesting money.

Using Vision Boards, Affirmations, and Scripting

Create a vision board that visually represents your desired financial reality. Include images, words, and symbols that evoke the feelings of abundance and prosperity. Craft empowering affirmations that align with your financial goals and repeat them daily. Utilize scripting, where you write your ideal financial story as if it has already happened.

These techniques program your subconscious mind for success.

Harnessing the Energy of the Law of Attraction

Engage in visualization exercises where you vividly imagine yourself already living in abundance. Create "money magnets" by placing symbols or objects associated with wealth and prosperity in your environment. Practice gratitude and appreciation for the money you have and the financial blessings in your life. Align your thoughts, emotions, and actions with the energy of abundance to attract more money.

By the end of this chapter, you will have learned practical money manifestation techniques, including creating a personalized money manifestation ritual, utilizing vision boards, affirmations, and scripting, and harnessing the energy of the Law of Attraction. These techniques will empower you to amplify your manifestation practice and align your energy with the frequency of financial abundance. Prepare to manifest money with intention, clarity, and focused energy.

CHAPTER 7: PRACTICAL STEPS FOR FINANCIAL SUCCESS

Manifesting money is not solely about visualization and mindset; it also requires practical steps and actions to support your financial success. In this chapter, we will explore practical strategies for budgeting, creating multiple streams of income, and investing to grow your wealth.

Developing Effective Budgeting and Financial Planning Skills

Master the art of budgeting to manage your finances effectively. Track your expenses, create a budget that aligns with your financial goals, and prioritize your spending. Set up a savings plan and automate your savings. Consider using budgeting apps or tools to help you stay organized and accountable.

Building Multiple Streams of Income

Diversify your income sources to enhance your financial stability and growth. Explore side hustles, freelancing opportunities, or creating passive income streams. Leverage your skills, expertise, and passions to create additional income streams. Consider investing in income-generating assets or starting a small business.

Multiple streams of income provide you with more financial security and opportunities for wealth accumulation.

Investing and Growing Your Wealth

Educate yourself about different investment options and strategies. Seek professional advice to make informed investment decisions. Explore avenues like stocks, real estate, mutual funds, or entrepreneurship. Understand the risks and rewards associated with each investment opportunity. By investing wisely, you can grow your wealth and create passive income streams.

By the end of this chapter, you will have gained practical insights into budgeting, creating multiple streams of income, and investing to grow your wealth. By combining practical steps with your manifestation practice, you will be on the path to financial success and abundance. Get ready to take control of your finances and build a solid financial future.

CHAPTER 8: MANIFESTING MONEY IN CAREER AND BUSINESS

In this chapter, we will explore how you can manifest money through your career and business endeavors. Whether you're seeking growth in your current job or pursuing entrepreneurial ventures, aligning your mindset and actions with abundance can propel you towards financial success.

Attracting Opportunities and Promotions in Your Career

Take intentional steps to advance your career and attract new opportunities. Network with professionals in your field, participate in relevant industry events, and invest in your professional development. Showcase your skills and expertise by taking on challenging projects and seeking feedback. Position yourself as a valuable asset to attract promotions and financial advancement.

Nurturing an Entrepreneurial Mindset for Business Success

Cultivate an entrepreneurial mindset if you're pursuing business ventures. Embrace innovation, take calculated risks, and persist through challenges. Surround yourself with a supportive network of like-minded individuals. Continuously learn and adapt to the ever-changing business landscape. Maintain a positive and resilient attitude, and believe in your ability to create financial success through your entrepreneurial endeavors.

Strategies for Attracting High-Paying Clients and Customers

Position your products or services as high-value offerings to attract high-paying clients or customers. Clearly define your target audience and understand their needs. Build relationships based on trust and provide exceptional customer experiences. Continuously improve your products or services and showcase the value they bring. By delivering outstanding quality, you can attract clients or customers who are willing to invest in your offerings.

By the end of this chapter, you will have gained insights into attracting opportunities and promotions in your career, nurturing an entrepreneurial mindset, and strategies for attracting high-paying clients or customers. By aligning your mindset and actions with abundance in your professional endeavors, you open the doors to greater financial success and prosperity. Prepare to manifest money through your career and business with purpose and intention.

CHAPTER 9: OVERCOMING FINANCIAL CHALLENGES AND BUILDING RESILIENCE

Life is filled with ups and downs, and the journey to financial abundance is no exception. In this chapter, we will explore the common financial challenges that many individuals face and delve into strategies for overcoming these obstacles while building resilience along the way. By developing a resilient mindset and implementing practical solutions, you will be better equipped to navigate through financial hardships and emerge stronger on the path to abundance.

Understanding Common Financial Challenges

Financial challenges come in various forms, and it's important to recognize and understand them. Whether it's debt, unexpected expenses, job loss, economic downturns, or unforeseen emergencies, these challenges can create stress and hinder your progress towards financial abundance. By acknowledging and gaining a deeper understanding of these challenges, you can develop effective strategies to overcome them.

Building Financial Resilience

Financial resilience is the ability to bounce back from setbacks and adapt to changing circumstances. It's about developing a strong foundation that can withstand the storms of life. In this section, we will explore strategies to build financial resilience, including:

- Emergency Funds: Building a financial safety net by setting aside funds specifically for emergencies. This provides a cushion to handle unexpected expenses without derailing your progress.
- Insurance Coverage: Protecting yourself and your assets through appropriate insurance policies, such as health insurance, home insurance, or disability insurance. Having the right coverage can mitigate financial risks in times of crisis.
- Smart Financial Planning: Creating a comprehensive financial plan that aligns with your goals and accounts for contingencies. This includes budgeting, setting financial milestones, and regularly reviewing and adjusting your plan as needed.
- Developing Multiple Income Streams: Diversifying your sources of income to reduce reliance on a single job or business. Exploring side hustles, freelancing opportunities, or investment options can provide additional streams of income and enhance your financial stability.

Cultivating a Positive Money Mindset During Challenges

Maintaining a positive money mindset is crucial when facing financial challenges. It's easy to succumb to fear, doubt, or scarcity thinking during difficult times, but shifting your mindset can make a significant difference. In this section, we will explore strategies to cultivate a positive money mindset, including:

- Self-Reflection and Awareness: Understanding your beliefs and attitudes towards money. Identify any limiting beliefs or negative patterns that may be hindering your progress. By becoming aware of these patterns, you can challenge and replace them with positive, empowering beliefs.
- Gratitude and Mindfulness: Practicing gratitude for what you have, even in challenging times. Cultivate mindfulness to stay present and focused on solutions rather than dwelling on problems. By shifting your focus to gratitude and abundance, you open yourself up to possibilities and attract positive outcomes.
- Seeking Support: Surrounding yourself with a supportive network of friends, family, or professionals who can offer guidance and encouragement. Sharing

your challenges and seeking advice from those who have overcome similar obstacles can provide valuable insights and motivation.

- Embracing Growth and Learning: Viewing financial challenges as opportunities for growth and learning. Instead of seeing setbacks as failures, see them as stepping stones towards greater resilience and wisdom. Embrace a growth mindset and seek out resources, books, courses, or mentors that can help you expand your financial knowledge and skills.

Overcoming financial challenges requires a combination of practical solutions and a resilient mindset. By understanding common challenges, building financial resilience, and cultivating a positive money mindset, you can navigate through difficult times and emerge stronger on your journey towards financial abundance. Remember that challenges are temporary, and with the right strategies and mindset, you can overcome them and continue on the path to manifesting the wealth and abundance you deserve.

CHAPTER 10: MANIFESTING MONEY IN CAREER AND BUSINESS

In the pursuit of financial abundance, it's essential to recognize the significance of giving back and sharing your wealth with others. This chapter explores the transformative power of generosity and the profound impact it can have on your journey towards abundance. By embracing the act of giving and contributing to the well-being of others, you not only enhance your own sense of fulfillment but also create a positive ripple effect in the world around you.

The Importance of Giving Back

Giving back is not just a moral obligation; it is an integral part of the abundance mindset. In this section, we will delve into the reasons why giving back is essential for your own growth and financial well-being. We will explore:

- Creating Meaning and Purpose: By giving back, you tap into a deeper sense of purpose and meaning in life. Contributing to causes or initiatives aligned with your values allows you to make a positive impact on the lives of others and contribute to the greater good.
- Cultivating Abundance Mentality: Giving back shifts your mindset from scarcity to

abundance. It reinforces the belief that there is always enough to go around and that you are part of a larger cycle of abundance. This mentality attracts more abundance into your own life.

- Fostering Connection and Community: Giving back connects you with like-minded individuals and communities who share your values. It fosters a sense of belonging and creates a supportive network that can uplift and inspire you on your journey.

Creating a Giving Mindset

Developing a giving mindset involves embracing generosity as a core value and making it an integral part of your life. In this section, we will explore practical strategies to cultivate a giving mindset, including:

- Aligning with Your Passions: Identify causes or areas of interest that resonate with you personally. When your giving aligns with your passions, it becomes more fulfilling and impactful.
- Volunteering Time and Skills: Giving back doesn't always have to involve financial contributions. Offer your time, expertise, or skills to organizations or individuals in need. Volunteering allows you to make a direct impact and connect with those you are helping.

- Charitable Donations: Explore different ways to contribute financially, such as making regular donations to charitable organizations, setting up a donor-advised fund, or establishing your own foundation. Understand the impact your donations can have and choose causes that align with your values.
- Supporting Local Businesses and Entrepreneurs: Extend your giving to the economic well-being of your community by supporting local businesses and entrepreneurs. By contributing to their success, you help create a thriving ecosystem that benefits everyone.

The Cycle of Abundance

In this section, we will delve into the concept of the cycle of abundance—the idea that giving and receiving are interconnected and feed into each other. We will explore:

- The Flow of Energy: Giving creates a flow of energy that expands and circulates. By sharing your abundance, you create space for more abundance to flow into your life.
- Receiving with Gratitude: Embrace the act of receiving with gratitude, recognizing that it allows others to experience the joy of giving. By graciously accepting help or

support when needed, you honor the interconnected nature of abundance.

- Intentional Giving: Approach giving with intention and mindfulness. Consider the impact you want to make and the legacy you want to leave behind. By being intentional, you can make a more meaningful and sustainable difference.

Giving back and sharing your abundance is a powerful way to manifest more wealth and create a positive impact in the world. By embracing the act of giving, cultivating a giving mindset, and understanding the cycle of abundance, you open yourself up to greater opportunities for growth, fulfillment, and financial success. Remember that by sharing your abundance, you contribute to a world where everyone can thrive, and you become a catalyst for positive change.

CHAPTER 11: LIVING A LIFE OF FINANCIAL ABUNDANCE

Congratulations! You have journeyed through the principles, practices, and mindset shifts necessary to manifest money and create a life of abundance. In this chapter, we will explore how to embody and live a life of financial abundance. This chapter will guide you in integrating the lessons learned, maintaining a prosperous mindset, and embracing the abundant lifestyle you have manifested.

Embodying Financial Abundance

Living a life of financial abundance goes beyond mere accumulation of wealth; it involves embodying the essence of abundance in all aspects of your being. In this section, we will delve into the key components of embodying financial abundance, including:

- Confidence and Self-Worth: Recognize and appreciate your own worthiness of financial abundance. Build self-confidence by acknowledging your accomplishments and embracing your unique strengths. As you radiate confidence, you attract opportunities and resources that align with your financial goals.
- Abundance Mindset: Maintain a positive and expansive mindset rooted in

abundance. Release any lingering scarcity thinking and embrace the belief that there is always more than enough for everyone. Cultivate gratitude for the wealth and opportunities that flow into your life, and celebrate the successes along your journey.

- Generosity and Sharing: Continue to embrace the act of giving and sharing your abundance with others. Share your wealth, resources, and knowledge with those around you, fostering a spirit of generosity and collaboration. As you give, you create a flow of abundance that comes back to you in unexpected ways.

Integrating Abundance Into Daily Life

Living a life of financial abundance requires intentional actions and habits that align with your newfound mindset and wealth. In this section, we will explore practical strategies to integrate abundance into your daily life, including:

- Conscious Spending: Align your spending habits with your values and financial goals. Practice mindful consumption by making intentional choices that support your overall well-being and financial abundance. Avoid impulsive purchases and cultivate a healthy relationship with money.

- Wealth Management: Take a proactive approach to managing your wealth. Create a solid financial plan that includes budgeting, saving, investing, and regularly reviewing your progress. Seek professional advice when needed and stay informed about financial trends and opportunities.
- Lifestyle Upgrades: As your financial abundance grows, you may choose to upgrade your lifestyle consciously. Make choices that bring joy, enhance your well-being, and align with your values. However, remember that material possessions alone do not define your abundance; it's the holistic experience of prosperity in all areas of life.
- Cultivating Abundant Relationships: Surround yourself with individuals who uplift and inspire you. Cultivate relationships built on trust, collaboration, and mutual support. Seek out mentors, like-minded communities, and opportunities for personal and professional growth.

Sustaining and Expanding Your Abundance

To sustain and expand your financial abundance, it's crucial to continue evolving and adapting to changing circumstances. In this section, we will explore strategies for sustaining and expanding your abundance, including:

- Lifelong Learning: Commit to ongoing personal and financial growth. Stay curious and open-minded, continuously expanding your knowledge and skills. Invest in education, attend seminars, read books, and seek guidance from experts in areas related to your financial goals.
- Embracing Innovation and Opportunities: Remain adaptable and open to new opportunities. Embrace innovation and technological advancements that can enhance your financial endeavors. Stay attuned to market trends and emerging industries that may present new avenues for wealth creation.
- Reviewing and Revising Goals: Regularly review and revise your financial goals. As you achieve milestones, set new targets that stretch your potential. Embrace the concept of lifelong goal-setting and understand that financial abundance is a dynamic and evolving journey.

Living a life of financial abundance is a journey that requires continuous growth, mindset shifts, and intentional actions. By embodying abundance, integrating it into your daily life, and sustaining and expanding your wealth, you create a foundation for long-term prosperity and fulfillment. Remember that true abundance encompasses not only financial wealth but also holistic well-being, purposeful living, and meaningful connections. Embrace the abundant lifestyle you have manifested and continue to create a positive impact in your life and the lives of others.

CHAPTER 12: MANIFESTING MONEY AS A FORCE FOR GOOD

As you have achieved financial abundance, it is essential to recognize the power and responsibility that comes with it. In this chapter, we will explore the concept of manifesting money as a force for good. This chapter will guide you in using your wealth to make a positive impact on the world, practicing conscious spending, and balancing financial success with social responsibility. By aligning your financial abundance with the greater good, you can create a legacy of positive change and contribute to a more prosperous and compassionate society.

Practicing Conscious Spending

Conscious spending is the intentional use of your financial resources to support your values and make a positive impact. In this section, we will explore strategies for practicing conscious spending, including:

- Aligning with Your Values: Reflect on your values and identify causes, organizations, and businesses that resonate with them. Direct your spending towards products and services that align with ethical and sustainable practices, supporting companies that prioritize social and environmental responsibility.

- Supporting Local and Small Businesses: Consider the impact of your spending on local economies and communities. Seek out local and small businesses, artisans, and entrepreneurs to support. By investing in local enterprises, you contribute to the growth and vitality of your community.
- Mindful Consumption: Practice mindful consumption by considering the long-term value and impact of your purchases. Ask yourself if an item truly aligns with your needs and if it will bring lasting satisfaction. Avoid impulsive or excessive spending, and instead prioritize quality, durability, and sustainability.
- Philanthropic Spending: Allocate a portion of your resources to philanthropy and charitable giving. Research and support causes and organizations that address pressing social and environmental issues. By consciously directing your financial resources to these causes, you become an agent of positive change.

Using Wealth to Make a Positive Impact

Financial abundance provides an opportunity to make a meaningful difference in the world. In this section, we will explore ways to use your wealth to make a positive impact, including:

- Philanthropy and Charitable Giving: Develop a philanthropic strategy that aligns with your values and desired impact. Consider establishing a foundation or contributing to existing charitable organizations. Regularly assess the impact of your giving and adjust your approach as needed.

- Impact Investing: Explore opportunities for impact investing, where you allocate your financial resources to projects or businesses that generate both financial returns and positive social or environmental outcomes. By investing in initiatives that align with your values, you can drive positive change while growing your wealth.

- Social Entrepreneurship: Consider starting or supporting social enterprises that aim to address societal challenges while maintaining financial sustainability. By combining business acumen with a social mission, you can create innovative solutions and empower communities.

- Mentorship and Education: Share your knowledge, skills, and resources with others through mentorship programs or educational initiatives. By empowering individuals, especially those from disadvantaged backgrounds, you contribute to their personal and financial growth.

Balancing Financial Success With Social Responsibility

Achieving financial success doesn't mean sacrificing social responsibility. It's about finding a balance between personal prosperity and contributing to the greater good. In this section, we will explore strategies for balancing financial success with social responsibility, including:

- Integrating Purpose in Business: If you are an entrepreneur or business leader, integrate purpose-driven practices into your business model. Consider the impact of your business operations on employees, customers, communities, and the environment. Strive for sustainable and socially responsible practices.
- Engaging in Advocacy: Use your financial influence to advocate for causes and policies that promote social justice, environmental sustainability, and economic equality. Support organizations and initiatives that work towards positive systemic change.
- Practicing Ethical Leadership: Lead by example by practicing ethical leadership in

your personal and professional life. Prioritize integrity, transparency, and fairness in your financial dealings. Inspire others to follow a similar path and create a culture of social responsibility.

Manifesting money as a force for good is a powerful way to create a lasting impact on society. By practicing conscious spending, using your wealth to make a positive impact, and balancing financial success with social responsibility, you contribute to a more compassionate and sustainable world. Embrace your role as a steward of financial abundance and recognize the transformative potential you possess to create positive change for the betterment of all.

CHAPTER 13: EMBRACING ABUNDANCE IN ALL AREAS OF LIFE

As you have embarked on the journey of manifesting money and creating a life of financial abundance, it's important to recognize that true prosperity encompasses more than just monetary wealth. This chapter explores the concept of embracing abundance in all areas of life. It delves into the interconnectedness of various aspects, such as health, relationships, personal growth, and spiritual well-being, and provides guidance on cultivating abundance holistically.

Nurturing Physical Well-being

Physical well-being forms the foundation for a prosperous life. In this section, we will explore strategies to nurture your physical health and well-being, including:

- Prioritizing Self-Care: Allocate time for self-care activities that support your physical well-being, such as regular exercise, nourishing meals, sufficient rest, and stress management. Remember that taking care of your body allows you to fully enjoy the abundance you have manifested.
- Mind-Body Connection: Recognize the intricate connection between your mind and body. Cultivate practices like

meditation, mindfulness, and yoga that promote a harmonious relationship between your physical and mental states. By nurturing this connection, you enhance your overall well-being.

- Seeking Professional Support: Consult with healthcare professionals, such as doctors, nutritionists, and therapists, to address any health concerns or imbalances. Prioritize preventive care and proactively manage your physical health to maintain vitality and energy.

Cultivating Fulfilling Relationships

Meaningful and fulfilling relationships contribute to a life of abundance. In this section, we will explore strategies for cultivating healthy and nourishing relationships, including:

- Authentic Connections: Foster relationships built on authenticity, trust, and mutual respect. Surround yourself with individuals who uplift and support you on your journey. Nurture connections with family, friends, and community members who contribute to your overall well-being.

- Effective Communication: Develop effective communication skills to express your needs, emotions, and boundaries clearly. Practice active listening and empathy to deepen understanding and connection with others. Healthy communication fosters harmonious relationships and enables you to manifest abundance together.

- Giving and Receiving Love: Embrace the power of love and compassion in your relationships. Cultivate a mindset of giving and receiving love unconditionally. Share your abundance, support others in their growth, and celebrate their successes. By nurturing loving relationships, you create a fertile ground for abundance to flourish.

Pursuing Personal Growth

Continual personal growth is a vital aspect of embracing abundance. In this section, we will explore strategies for personal growth and self-development, including:

- Lifelong Learning: Maintain a curious and open mindset, and commit to lifelong learning. Engage in activities that expand your knowledge, skills, and perspectives. Pursue education, attend workshops or seminars, read books, and seek mentors who inspire and challenge you.
- Embracing Change and Resilience: Embrace change as an opportunity for growth and transformation. Develop resilience in the face of challenges and

setbacks. See obstacles as valuable lessons and stepping stones toward greater abundance. Embracing change empowers you to adapt and thrive in an ever-evolving world.

- Setting and Achieving Meaningful Goals: Continuously set and pursue meaningful goals aligned with your values and passions. Break them down into actionable steps, track your progress, and celebrate milestones along the way. By achieving personal goals, you create a sense of fulfillment and expand your capacity for abundance.

Nurturing Spiritual Well-being

Spiritual well-being provides a sense of purpose, connection, and inner peace. In this section, we will explore strategies for nurturing your spiritual well-being, including:

- Cultivating Mindfulness and Presence: Practice mindfulness and present-moment awareness to deepen your spiritual connection. Engage in activities that bring you joy, peace, and a sense of transcendence. Connect with nature, meditate, journal, or engage in spiritual practices that resonate with you.
- Connecting to Something Greater: Explore and nurture your connection to a higher

power, whether through religious or spiritual practices. Engage in acts of gratitude, prayer, or contemplation to deepen your spiritual connection and tap into a source of guidance and abundance.

- Aligning Actions with Values: Ensure that your actions align with your core values and spiritual beliefs. Act with integrity, compassion, and kindness in all aspects of your life. By living in alignment with your values, you invite greater abundance and spiritual fulfillment.

Embracing abundance in all areas of life is a holistic approach to living a fulfilled and prosperous existence. By nurturing physical well-being, cultivating fulfilling relationships, pursuing personal growth, and nurturing spiritual well-being, you create a solid foundation for a life of abundance. Remember that true prosperity encompasses more than just financial wealth—it is the integration of health, relationships, personal growth, and spiritual fulfillment. Embrace the interconnectedness of these aspects and continue to manifest abundance in all areas of your life.

CHAPTER 14: SUSTAINING AND EXPANDING YOUR ABUNDANCE

Having cultivated a life of abundance, it is crucial to sustain and expand your prosperity over time. This chapter explores strategies for sustaining and expanding your abundance, providing guidance on maintaining a prosperous mindset, adapting to changing circumstances, and continually growing your wealth. By implementing these principles, you will create a solid foundation for long-term prosperity and the ability to thrive in an ever-changing world.

Cultivating a Prosperous Mindset

Maintaining a prosperous mindset is essential for sustaining and expanding your abundance. In this section, we will explore strategies to cultivate and reinforce a prosperous mindset, including:

- Gratitude and Appreciation: Practice gratitude for the abundance already present in your life. Regularly acknowledge and appreciate the wealth, opportunities, and blessings that have come your way. Gratitude cultivates a positive outlook and attracts more abundance into your life.
- Positive Self-Talk and Affirmations: Monitor and consciously shape your thoughts and self-talk. Replace limiting

beliefs and negative self-talk with empowering affirmations and positive statements about your abundance. By rewiring your mind for success, you create a fertile ground for continued prosperity.

- Visualization and Manifestation: Utilize visualization techniques to vividly imagine your desired outcomes and abundance. Engage all your senses and immerse yourself in the experience of already having achieved your goals. Visualizing and manifesting abundance helps align your actions with your intentions.

Adapting to Changing Circumstances

To sustain and expand your abundance, it is essential to adapt to changing circumstances. In this section, we will explore strategies for adapting and thriving in the face of change, including:

- Flexibility and Resilience: Cultivate a mindset of flexibility and adaptability. Embrace change as an opportunity for growth and expansion rather than a setback. Develop resilience to navigate challenges and setbacks confidently, knowing that they are stepping stones to greater abundance.
- Continuous Learning and Skill Development: Commit to lifelong learning

and skill development. Stay curious and open-minded, seeking opportunities to enhance your knowledge and expertise. Embrace new technologies, industry trends, and innovations to stay ahead and seize new opportunities.

- Networking and Collaboration: Build a strong network of like-minded individuals who can support and inspire you on your journey. Seek out collaboration opportunities to leverage collective knowledge and resources. By surrounding yourself with a supportive community, you create a resilient ecosystem for sustained abundance.

Growing Your Wealth

Expanding your wealth is a natural progression of your abundant mindset and actions. In this section, we will explore strategies for growing your wealth, including:

- Strategic Investing: Continue to invest your resources strategically. Educate yourself about different investment vehicles, diversify your portfolio, and seek professional advice when needed. Be mindful of risks and rewards, and make informed decisions that align with your financial goals.

- Entrepreneurship and Business Expansion: Explore entrepreneurial opportunities and consider expanding your business ventures. Leverage your expertise, resources, and network to identify and pursue new avenues for wealth creation. Embrace innovation and stay adaptable in the ever-evolving business landscape.
- Multiple Streams of Income: Diversify your income sources to create stability and long-term wealth. Explore opportunities for passive income, such as real estate investments, royalties, or online ventures. By generating multiple streams of income, you increase your financial security and create room for further expansion.

Sustaining and expanding your abundance requires a proactive and growth-oriented approach. By cultivating a prosperous mindset, adapting to changing circumstances, and continually growing your wealth, you create a solid foundation for sustained prosperity. Embrace the principles outlined in this chapter and recognize that abundance is not a static state—it is a dynamic and evolving journey. Stay committed to your goals, be open to new opportunities, and continue to expand your wealth and impact in the world.

CHAPTER 15: EMBRACING ABUNDANCE BEYOND MONEY

Throughout this book, we have explored the process of manifesting money and creating a life of financial abundance. However, true abundance extends far beyond monetary wealth. This chapter delves into the concept of embracing abundance beyond money, focusing on the enrichment of experiences, relationships, personal fulfillment, and overall well-being. By broadening our perspective of abundance, we can cultivate a more holistic and fulfilling life.

Embracing Experiences

Abundance goes hand in hand with enriching experiences that bring joy, fulfillment, and growth. In this section, we will explore strategies for embracing experiential abundance, including:

- Exploring Passions and Hobbies: Dedicate time and energy to pursuing activities that ignite your passion and bring you joy. Engage in hobbies, artistic endeavors, or sports that fuel your creativity and allow you to fully immerse yourself in the present moment. Embracing your passions brings a sense of fulfillment and expands your overall abundance.

- Seeking Adventure and Travel: Embrace the opportunity to explore new places, cultures, and experiences. Travel broadens your horizons, exposes you to diverse perspectives, and creates lasting memories. By venturing into the unknown and embracing adventure, you invite abundance and growth into your life.
- Embracing Mindful Presence: Practice being fully present in each moment, savoring the richness of life's simple pleasures. Engage your senses, notice the beauty around you, and appreciate the small moments that often go unnoticed. By cultivating mindful presence, you tap into the abundant richness of everyday life.

Nurturing Relationships and Connections

Meaningful relationships and connections form an essential aspect of abundant living. In this section, we will explore strategies for nurturing and embracing abundance in relationships, including:

- Cultivating Authentic Connections: Foster relationships built on trust, authenticity, and mutual support. Surround yourself with people who uplift and inspire you, and reciprocate by being a source of positivity and encouragement. Nurturing authentic connections expands your social abundance and enriches your life.

- Practicing Love and Kindness: Embrace love and kindness as guiding principles in your relationships. Practice compassion, empathy, and understanding towards others. Show appreciation and gratitude for the people in your life. By nurturing loving relationships, you create a reservoir of abundant joy and support.

- Investing in Family and Community: Prioritize your relationships with family members and actively contribute to your community. Support and nurture your familial bonds, creating a sense of belonging and support. Engage in acts of service and contribute to the well-being of your community, fostering a collective abundance.

Pursuing Personal Fulfillment

True abundance involves pursuing personal fulfillment and aligning with your life's purpose. In this section, we will explore strategies for embracing personal fulfillment and purpose, including:

- Discovering Your Life's Purpose: Reflect on your passions, talents, and values to identify your life's purpose. Explore ways to align your work, hobbies, and activities with your purpose. By living in alignment with your purpose, you invite a deep sense of fulfillment and abundance into your life.

- Cultivating Self-Love and Self-Care: Prioritize self-love and self-care as integral aspects of personal fulfillment. Nurture your physical, mental, and emotional well-being. Practice self-compassion, set healthy boundaries, and engage in activities that promote self-growth and personal development.

- Contributing to the Greater Good: Embrace the opportunity to make a positive impact on the world. Identify ways to use your skills, resources, and influence to contribute to causes that resonate with your values. By serving others and contributing to the greater good, you experience a profound sense of abundance and purpose.

Embracing abundance beyond money is a transformative journey that expands our perspective and enriches our lives. By embracing experiential abundance, nurturing meaningful relationships, and pursuing personal fulfillment, we unlock the true essence of abundance. Embrace the richness of life's experiences, foster deep connections, and align with your purpose to create a life of holistic abundance and fulfillment.

Remember, true abundance encompasses all aspects of our being and extends far beyond monetary wealth.

CHAPTER 16: CULTIVATING A LASTING LEGACY OF ABUNDANCE

As you have journeyed through the process of manifesting money and embracing abundance, it is essential to consider the legacy you will leave behind. This chapter explores the concept of cultivating a lasting legacy of abundance, focusing on creating a positive impact that extends beyond your own lifetime. By consciously shaping your legacy, you can leave a profound imprint on the world and inspire future generations to embrace abundance and create positive change.

Defining Your Legacy

To cultivate a lasting legacy of abundance, it is important to first define what that means to you. In this section, we will explore strategies for defining your legacy, including:

- Clarifying Your Values: Reflect on your core values and beliefs. Identify the principles and ideals that are most important to you and align with your vision of abundance. Understanding your values serves as a compass for shaping your legacy.
- Identifying Your Passions: Explore your passions and areas of interest that inspire you. Consider how you can incorporate these passions into your legacy, utilizing

them as catalysts for positive change and impact.

- Envisioning Your Impact: Visualize the impact you want to have on the world. Imagine the changes you want to see and the legacy you want to leave behind. Envision how your abundance can be a force for good, inspiring others and making a lasting difference.

Creating a Ripple Effect

To cultivate a lasting legacy, it is important to create a ripple effect of abundance and positive change. In this section, we will explore strategies for creating a ripple effect, including:

- Mentoring and Empowering Others: Share your knowledge, experiences, and resources with others. Mentor and empower individuals who can benefit from your guidance and support. By lifting others up and helping them embrace their own abundance, you create a ripple effect of positive change.

- Philanthropy and Social Impact: Channel your abundance towards philanthropic endeavors and social impact initiatives. Support causes that align with your values and have the potential to create meaningful change. By leveraging your resources for the greater good, you create a ripple effect of abundance and inspire others to do the same.

- Collaboration and Partnerships: Seek opportunities for collaboration and partnerships with like-minded individuals and organizations. By joining forces, you can amplify your impact and create a collective ripple effect of abundance and positive change.

Inspiring Future Generations

To create a lasting legacy, it is essential to inspire and empower future generations to embrace abundance and create positive change. In this section, we will explore strategies for inspiring future generations, including:

- Education and Mentorship Programs: Support educational initiatives and mentorship programs that empower young individuals to embrace abundance and develop the skills necessary for success. By investing in the next generation, you create a ripple effect of abundance that extends far into the future.

- Leading by Example: Be a role model for embracing abundance and living a purpose-driven life. Demonstrate through your actions the power of abundance and the impact it can have on individuals and communities. By leading by example, you inspire others to follow in your footsteps and create their own legacies of abundance.

- Storytelling and Sharing Wisdom: Share your journey, experiences, and lessons learned with future generations. Use storytelling as a powerful tool to convey the principles of abundance and inspire others to cultivate their own legacies. By sharing wisdom and stories of abundance, you ignite a spark of inspiration and empowerment in the hearts of others.

Cultivating a lasting legacy of abundance is a conscious and intentional endeavor. By defining your legacy, creating a ripple effect of positive change, and inspiring future generations, you can leave a profound imprint on the world. Embrace the opportunity to shape a legacy that reflects your values, passions, and vision of abundance. Through your actions, generosity, and commitment to making a difference, you can create a legacy that extends far beyond your own lifetime, leaving a legacy of abundance for generations to come.

CHAPTER 17: EMBRACING ABUNDANCE AS A WAY OF LIFE

Throughout this book, we have explored various strategies and principles for manifesting money and embracing abundance. In this chapter, we shift our focus to the idea of embracing abundance as a way of life—a mindset and approach that permeates every aspect of our existence. By integrating abundance into our daily lives, we can experience sustained joy, fulfillment, and prosperity.

Embracing an Abundance Mindset

At the core of living an abundant life is cultivating an abundance mindset. In this section, we will explore strategies for embracing an abundance mindset, including:

- Shifting from Scarcity to Abundance: Challenge scarcity-based thinking and replace it with a mindset of abundance. Recognize that the universe is abundant and holds infinite possibilities. Shift your focus from limitations to opportunities, from lack to abundance.

- Practicing Gratitude and Appreciation: Cultivate a habit of gratitude and appreciation for the abundance already present in your life. Regularly acknowledge and express gratitude for the blessings, experiences, and relationships that bring joy and fulfillment. Gratitude amplifies abundance.

- Embracing Positive Self-Talk: Monitor your thoughts and self-talk, ensuring they align with abundance and empowerment. Replace self-limiting beliefs with positive affirmations and statements that reinforce your abundance. Embrace the power of positive thinking.

Integrating Abundance Into Daily Rituals

Living an abundant life requires intentional integration of abundance into our daily rituals and practices. In this section, we will explore strategies for integrating abundance into daily life, including:

- Morning Abundance Rituals: Begin each day with rituals that cultivate an abundant mindset. Practice gratitude, set intentions aligned with abundance, visualize your desired outcomes, and engage in positive affirmations. These rituals set the tone for a day filled with abundance.
- Abundance Journaling: Incorporate abundance journaling into your routine. Write down your gratitude list, reflect on the abundance you've experienced, and visualize your future abundance. Journaling allows you to reinforce your

abundance mindset and focus your energy on what you want to manifest.

- Acts of Abundant Giving: Embrace the practice of giving and generosity. Find opportunities to give back to others, whether through acts of kindness, charitable donations, or sharing your resources. Giving amplifies abundance and creates a cycle of reciprocity.

Nurturing a Balanced Abundant Life

Living an abundant life involves nurturing a balanced existence that encompasses all areas of our being. In this section, we will explore strategies for nurturing a balanced abundant life, including:

- Health and Well-being: Prioritize your physical and mental well-being. Maintain a healthy lifestyle, engage in regular exercise, nourish your body with nutritious food, and practice self-care. A healthy body and mind form the foundation for an abundant life.
- Relationships and Connection: Cultivate meaningful relationships and connections. Prioritize quality time with loved ones, practice active listening, and foster deep connections. Healthy relationships contribute to our overall sense of abundance and fulfillment.

- Personal Growth and Learning: Embrace personal growth and lifelong learning. Pursue activities, courses, and experiences that expand your knowledge, skills, and perspectives. Continual growth and learning enhance our sense of abundance and open doors to new opportunities.

Embracing abundance as a way of life is a transformative journey that transcends mere financial wealth. By cultivating an abundance mindset, integrating abundance into our daily rituals, and nurturing a balanced abundant life, we unlock the full potential of living an abundant existence. Embrace the principles outlined in this chapter and strive to make abundance a fundamental aspect of your being. As you do so, you will experience a profound shift in your perception, actions, and outcomes, leading to a life of sustained joy, fulfillment, and prosperity.

CHAPTER 18: EMBRACING THE EVOLUTION OF ABUNDANCE IN THE DIGITAL AGE

In today's rapidly evolving digital age, the concept of abundance is taking on new dimensions. This chapter explores the intersection of abundance and technology, highlighting how digital advancements have transformed the way we manifest and experience abundance. From the rise of online entrepreneurship to the possibilities of cryptocurrency and virtual economies, this chapter delves into the opportunities and challenges presented by the digital landscape.

The Digital Entrepreneur

The digital age has opened up unprecedented opportunities for individuals to embrace entrepreneurship and create abundance through online platforms. In this section, we will explore the key aspects of being a digital entrepreneur, including:

- Leveraging Online Platforms: Harness the power of online platforms, such as e-commerce websites, social media, and digital marketplaces, to showcase your products or services. The digital landscape allows for global reach, enabling entrepreneurs to connect with a vast audience and create abundance on a larger scale.

- Embracing Remote Work and Digital Nomadism: Explore the flexibility and freedom of remote work. Embrace the digital nomad lifestyle, leveraging technology to work from anywhere in the world. This lifestyle allows for the integration of work and travel, expanding opportunities for abundance and personal growth.

- Building Digital Products and Services: Create and monetize digital products and services, such as e-books, online courses, software applications, or consulting services. The digital realm provides a platform for scalable and profitable offerings that can generate abundant income streams.

The Rise of Cryptocurrency

Cryptocurrency has emerged as a disruptive force in the financial landscape, presenting new possibilities for abundance and wealth creation. In this section, we will explore the world of cryptocurrency and its implications, including:

- Understanding Blockchain Technology: Gain a foundational understanding of blockchain technology, the underlying infrastructure behind cryptocurrencies.

Explore its potential for revolutionizing various industries and enabling secure, decentralized transactions.

- Investing and Trading Cryptocurrency: Explore the opportunities and risks associated with investing and trading cryptocurrencies. Understand the basics of cryptocurrency markets, strategies for investment, and the importance of responsible risk management.

- Exploring Decentralized Finance (DeFi): Discover the concept of decentralized finance (DeFi) and the transformative potential it holds. Learn about decentralized lending, staking, yield farming, and other innovative financial applications that empower individuals to participate in the financial ecosystem.

Navigating the Digital Landscape

Living in the digital age comes with its unique challenges and considerations. In this section, we will explore strategies for navigating the digital landscape while maintaining a healthy and balanced approach to abundance, including:

- Digital Well-being: Practice digital well-being by setting boundaries, managing screen time, and prioritizing offline experiences. Cultivate mindfulness and intentional technology use to avoid the pitfalls of information overload and digital distractions.

- Cybersecurity and Privacy: Understand the importance of cybersecurity and safeguarding your digital assets. Learn about best practices for protecting personal and financial information online, including the use of strong passwords, two-factor authentication, and encrypted communication.

- Ethical Considerations: Reflect on the ethical implications of the digital age and the responsible use of technology. Embrace ethical practices in online entrepreneurship, data privacy, and digital interactions. Strive to create abundance while upholding values of integrity, transparency, and social responsibility.

The digital age has brought about a profound shift in how we manifest and experience abundance. By embracing the opportunities presented by online entrepreneurship, cryptocurrency, and the digital landscape at large, we can create new avenues for abundance and financial prosperity. However, it is important to navigate the digital landscape with mindfulness, maintaining a healthy balance and upholding ethical principles. By embracing the evolution of abundance in the digital age, we can harness the full potential of technology to manifest abundance and create a prosperous future.

75

CHAPTER 19: CULTIVATING ABUNDANCE IN CHALLENGING TIMES

Life is full of ups and downs, and there are times when we face challenges that may test our ability to cultivate abundance. This chapter explores the art of cultivating abundance in the face of adversity, providing guidance and strategies for maintaining a positive mindset and manifesting abundance even during challenging times. By embracing resilience and adapting to circumstances, we can find opportunities for growth, learn valuable lessons, and ultimately continue on the path of abundance.

Embracing Resilience

Resilience is the key to navigating challenging times and maintaining an abundant mindset. In this section, we will explore strategies for embracing resilience, including:

- Developing a Growth Mindset: Cultivate a growth mindset that sees challenges as opportunities for learning and growth. Embrace the belief that setbacks are temporary and can be overcome with perseverance and adaptability.
- Practicing Self-Compassion: Show kindness and understanding to yourself during difficult times. Practice self-care,

engage in activities that bring you joy and relaxation, and seek support from loved ones or professionals when needed.

- Finding Silver Linings: Look for the silver linings amidst challenging situations. Focus on the lessons learned, the personal growth that emerges, and the new opportunities that may arise as a result of adversity.

Adapting and Innovating

During challenging times, it is crucial to adapt and innovate in order to thrive. In this section, we will explore strategies for adapting and innovating, including:

- Assessing and Adjusting Goals: Evaluate your goals and priorities in light of the current circumstances. Be open to adjusting your plans and strategies as needed to align with the changing landscape. Seek new opportunities that may arise and explore innovative approaches.
- Embracing Digital Solutions: Leverage the power of technology and digital platforms to adapt your business or career. Explore new ways of reaching your audience or customers through online channels, virtual events, or remote work opportunities.

- Seeking Collaborations and Partnerships: Forge collaborations and partnerships with like-minded individuals or organizations. By joining forces, you can pool resources, share knowledge, and create innovative solutions to overcome challenges together.

Cultivating Gratitude and Positivity

Maintaining a positive mindset and cultivating gratitude are essential during challenging times. In this section, we will explore strategies for cultivating gratitude and positivity, including:

- Daily Gratitude Practice: Cultivate a daily gratitude practice by reflecting on the things you are grateful for, no matter how small. This practice shifts your focus towards abundance and reminds you of the positive aspects of your life.
- Surrounding Yourself with Positivity: Surround yourself with positive influences, whether it be uplifting books, motivational podcasts, supportive friends, or inspirational role models. Choose to engage in activities that bring you joy and foster positivity.
- Practicing Mindfulness: Embrace mindfulness as a tool to stay present and grounded during challenging times. Practice meditation, deep breathing

exercises, or other mindfulness techniques to cultivate inner peace and resilience.

Cultivating abundance in challenging times requires resilience, adaptability, and a positive mindset. By embracing resilience, adapting to circumstances, and maintaining gratitude and positivity, we can navigate through difficult situations and continue on the path of abundance. Remember that challenges present opportunities for growth, and by cultivating an abundant mindset, we can manifest abundance even in the face of adversity.

CHAPTER 20: CULTIVATING ABUNDANCE IN CHALLENGING TIME S

In our pursuit of manifesting money and abundance, it is essential to consider the long-term sustainability of our wealth. This chapter delves into the concept of sustainable wealth, exploring how we can create and manage our financial resources in a way that ensures not only our own prosperity but also the well-being of future generations and the planet. By adopting a holistic approach to wealth creation and aligning our financial practices with sustainability principles, we can embark on a journey of sustainable wealth that benefits both ourselves and the world around us.

Defining Sustainable Wealth

In this section, we will define sustainable wealth and explore its components, including:

- Financial Prosperity: Sustainable wealth involves achieving financial prosperity and abundance through conscious and responsible financial practices. It encompasses building wealth, managing debt, and making wise investment decisions.
- Environmental Stewardship: Sustainable wealth recognizes the importance of

environmental conservation and minimizing our ecological footprint. It involves considering the environmental impact of our financial choices and supporting sustainable business practices.

- Social Responsibility: Sustainable wealth incorporates social responsibility by promoting fair and ethical practices, supporting community development, and contributing to social causes. It emphasizes creating shared value for both individuals and society.

Investing in Sustainable Businesses

Investing in sustainable businesses is a key aspect of sustainable wealth creation. In this section, we will explore strategies for investing in sustainable companies, including:

- Sustainable Investment Principles: Learn about sustainable investment principles, such as Environmental, Social, and Governance (ESG) criteria, impact investing, and socially responsible investing (SRI). Understand how these principles can guide your investment decisions.

- Research and Due Diligence: Conduct thorough research and due diligence when selecting sustainable investment opportunities. Look for companies that align with your values, demonstrate sustainable practices, and have a positive social and environmental impact.

- Diversification and Risk Management: Apply diversification strategies and risk management techniques to your investment portfolio. Spread your investments across different asset classes and industries to mitigate risks and optimize returns.

Philanthropy and Giving Back

Philanthropy plays a crucial role in the journey of sustainable wealth. In this section, we will explore the importance of philanthropy and strategies for giving back, including:

- Strategic Philanthropy: Develop a strategic philanthropy plan that aligns with your values and desired impact. Identify causes or organizations that resonate with you and allocate resources, whether financial or non-financial, to support their work.

- Leveraging Skills and Expertise: Go beyond monetary contributions and leverage your skills, expertise, and networks to make a meaningful impact. Consider volunteering, mentorship, or pro bono work to contribute to social and environmental causes.

- Legacy Planning: Incorporate philanthropy into your legacy planning. Explore options such as creating a charitable foundation, establishing donor-advised funds, or including charitable bequests in your estate planning to ensure your philanthropic efforts continue beyond your lifetime.

Conscious Consumption and Lifestyle Choices

Sustainable wealth extends beyond financial practices to encompass conscious consumption and lifestyle choices. In this section, we will explore strategies for aligning our lifestyle with sustainability principles, including:

- Responsible Spending: Practice responsible spending by considering the environmental and social impact of the products and services you consume. Opt for sustainable, ethically sourced, and eco-friendly options whenever possible.
- Minimalism and Mindful Consumption: Embrace minimalism and mindful consumption by decluttering your life and focusing on experiences rather than material possessions. Prioritize quality over quantity and make conscious choices that align with your values.
- Sustainable Living Practices: Adopt sustainable living practices such as energy

conservation, waste reduction, and eco-friendly alternatives. Incorporate sustainability into your daily routines, from transportation choices to home energy management.

The journey of sustainable wealth invites us to consider the long-term impact of our financial choices, not only on our own well-being but also on the well-being of the planet and future generations. By embracing sustainable wealth principles, investing in sustainable businesses, practicing philanthropy, and making conscious consumption and lifestyle choices, we can create a legacy of abundance that is built on sustainability and social responsibility. Let us embark on this journey with the intention of leaving a positive and lasting impact on the world.

EPILOGUE: EMBRACING THE ABUNDANCE WITHIN

Congratulations on completing this transformative journey of manifesting money and embracing abundance. Throughout this book, we have explored the principles, practices, and mindset shifts necessary to manifest money and create a life of prosperity. From understanding the power of intention and visualization to exploring the role of gratitude, mindset, and conscious action, you have gained valuable insights and tools to manifest money and abundance in your life.

Remember that the journey of manifesting money goes beyond the acquisition of wealth. It is about aligning our financial goals with our values, finding fulfillment in our pursuits, and making a positive impact on the world. As you continue your path towards abundance, I encourage you to reflect on the lessons you have learned and integrate them into your daily life.

Embrace the abundance that resides within you. Cultivate a mindset of abundance that transcends material wealth and encompasses love, joy, health, and meaningful connections. Recognize the abundance of opportunities that surround you, and trust in your ability to seize them.

As you navigate the ever-changing landscape of finance, technology, and social dynamics, remember to stay true to your values and embrace sustainability and social responsibility. Be conscious of the impact your financial choices have on the environment, society, and future generations. Use your wealth as a force for good, supporting causes and initiatives that align with your values and contribute to a better world.

Continue to nurture your relationship with money. Maintain a healthy balance between financial growth and personal well-being. Practice gratitude, for it is through gratitude that we open ourselves to receiving more abundance. Cultivate an abundant mindset, letting go of scarcity and fear, and embracing a belief in limitless possibilities.

Remember that true abundance comes not just from the external world but from within. Nurture your inner abundance through self-care, self-love, and personal growth. Embrace the journey of self-discovery and self-empowerment, for it is from this place of inner abundance that you can manifest and attract external abundance effortlessly.

As you conclude this book, carry the wisdom and insights gained on your journey. Embrace the responsibility that comes with abundance and use it to create a positive impact on your life and the lives of others. Trust in your ability to manifest money and abundance, and always remember that you are deserving of all the abundance that the universe has to offer.

May your path be filled with prosperity, joy, and fulfillment. May you continue to manifest money and abundance in alignment with your highest values and purpose. Embrace the abundant life that awaits you and let your journey of abundance inspire and uplift others.

Thank you for joining me on this transformative journey, and I wish you a life filled with abundance in all its forms.

With love and abundance,

Jeff Hill

www.ingramcontent.com/pod-product-compliance
Lightning Source LLC
Chambersburg PA
CBHW050557160726
48003CB00002B/932